Inflation and Variable Interest

Mohammed Azzam

Published by Mohammed Azzam, 2018.

While every precaution has been taken in the preparation of this book, the publisher assumes no responsibility for errors or omissions, or for damages resulting from the use of the information contained herein.

INFLATION AND VARIABLE INTEREST

First edition. October 6, 2018.

Copyright © 2018 Mohammed Azzam.

Written by Mohammed Azzam.

Also by Mohammed Azzam

Inflation and Variable Interest
Virtual Reality and Augmented Reality Safety Rules
Known Facts of Time Travel

Watch for more at https://books2read.com/ap/
R3Lm35/Mohammed-Azzam.

Preface

Is export the best solution for smooth economy? Should America for example go for more export and less import as the magical economic remedy? This book discusses these questions and tries to find the best answers for them. This book discusses currency flotation: what is it? It introduces some of currency flotation features! This book tries to find an answer to why currency flotation? By comparing both fixed exchange rate system and the floating exchange rate system, then it discusses their advantages and disadvantages, also this book introduces the relationship between export and currency fluctuations. This book discusses the advantages and disadvantages of inflation and the relationship between inflation rate and interest rate, it also explains how to limit inflation. Finally, this book introduces a closed loop automatic control system on inflation rate!

This automatic control system on inflation rate is an economic theory called "Inflation Rate Control Loop" theory. This theory introduces an alternative way for devaluation of currency to increase inflation rate, which is important for Euro zone! This book explains this theory, the obstacles that are faced while applying it to economic system and how to overcome such obstacles in a short description. This book talks about this theory's benefits in short description too.

Finally, I wish for someone to find this book useful! Especially "Inflation Rate Control Loop" theory.

Currency Flotation

What's currency flotation? A floating currency is a monetary system that is not backed by gold or assets and tends to fluctuate in value due to supply and market expectations. Its value is also determined by global demand and the level of foreign reserves. Floating currencies have a floating exchange rate, which changes based on the demand and supply mechanisms of the foreign exchange market which is called Forex. This contrasts with a fixed exchange rate monetary system, in which the government entirely or predominantly determines the rate. When the demand for a currency is high, the currency appreciates in value, thus impacting the country's exports. A strong currency shifts consumer to a cheaper currency, thus lowering the demand for the exported goods. In the long run, exporters must lower their prices to attract consumers, thus lowering their profits and facing the risk of going out of business. Conversely, when the demand for a currency is low, the currency depreciates in value, thus impacting the country's importers. A weak currency makes imported goods expensive. Therefore, consumers buy domestic goods, thus stimulating the domestic economy. In both cases, a floating currency tends to be volatile.

What's currency devaluation? In modern monetary policy, a devaluation is an official lowering of the value of a country's currency within a fixed exchange rate system, by which the monetary authority formally sets a new fixed rate with respect to a foreign reference currency or currency basket.

What's currency revaluation? Revaluation is a change in a price of a good or product, or especially of a currency, in which case it is specifically an official rise of the value of the currency in relation to a foreign currency in a fixed exchange rate system. ... In contrast, a devaluation is an official reduction in the value of the currency.

What's inflation? Inflation is the rate at which the general level of prices for goods and services is rising and, consequently, the purchasing power of currency is falling. Central banks attempt to limit inflation and

INFLATION AND VARIABLE INTEREST

avoid deflation in order to keep the economy running smoothly. The measure of inflation over time is referred to as the inflation rate.

What's deflation? Deflation is a decrease in the general price level of goods and services. Deflation occurs when the inflation rate falls below 0%, which is a negative inflation rate. Inflation reduces the value of currency over time, but deflation increases it.

What's the catch? The catch is devaluation of local currency leads to increase inflation rate as devaluation of local currency means price increase for goods, while revaluation of local currency leads to decrease inflation rate, as revaluation of local currency means price decrease for goods. This decrease of inflation rate could let the inflation rate falls below 0%, in other words decrease of inflation rate could cause deflation.

Today, most of the widely traded currencies, such as the US dollar, the Euro, the British pound or the Japanese yen, have a floating exchange rate. However, central banks often raise concerns about the implications of adopting a floating exchange rate and how floating currencies can affect global foreign investment and monetary policies.

The main argument against floating exchange rates is that they enable monetary policy makers to use the exchange rate to achieve a competitive advantage. The strong US dollar may appreciate or depreciate, yet the monetary policy makers use it to stabilize the general price level.

This concludes currency flotation leads to currency fluctuations. A little bit of inflation is good for economic growth around 2-3% a year. But, when prices begin to fall after an economic downturn, deflation may set in causing an even deeper and more severe crisis. As prices fall, production slows, and inventories are liquidated. Demand drops and unemployment increases.

Why Currency Flotation?

Let us make an in-depth study of the advantages and disadvantages of the fixed exchange rate system and the floating exchange rate system.

Advantages of fixed exchange rate system:

First, Elimination of Uncertainty and Risk:

This is the necessary condition for an orderly and steady growth of trade demands stability in exchange rate. Any undue fluctuations in exchange rate cause problems to the plans and programs of both exporters and imports.

In other words, incomes of export-earners and the cost of imports of the importers tend to become uncertain if the exchange rate fluctuates. This uncertainty can be removed by a fixed exchange rate method. Further, the risks associated with international trade and investment get minimized largely if exchange rates are not allowed to vary.

Second, Speculation Deterred:

As exchange rate remains unchanged for a fairly long period of time, people expect that such rate would not change in the immediate future. This then eliminates speculation in the foreign exchange market.

Further, as stability in the exchange rate over longish period eliminates the threat of speculation, it discourages the flight of capital. In a world of free fluctuating exchange rate, the danger of the flight of capital is rather high as this kind of exchange rate induces people to speculate. As exchange rates remain fixed, traders have a sense of confidence that international payments can be made safely without the danger of losses.

Third, Prevention of Depreciation of Currency:

In poor developing countries, they experience balance of payments difficulties of a permanent type. Under the circumstances, any frequent changes in exchange rate will tend to aggravate the balance of payments crisis, for example, continuous depreciation of home currency in terms of currencies of other countries. In other words, unstable exchange rates result in depreciation of currencies. This can be prevented by the stable exchange rate.

Fourth, Adoption of Responsible Macroeconomic Policies:

Stable exchange rate system prevents government from adopting irresponsible macro-economic policies like devaluation of currencies. Above all, under the fixed exchange rate system, deflationary policies can even be pursued to tide over the balance of payments deficit, even without bringing any change in domestic policies.

Fifth, Attraction of Foreign Investment:

Exchange rate stability may encourage foreigners to perk their investible funds in a country. If the exchange rate changes rather frequently, it will deter them from investing in a country. Of course, such foreign investment having multiplier effect leads to higher economic growth.

Sixth, Anti-inflationary:

Fixed exchange rate system is anti-inflationary in character. If exchange rate can decline, import goods tend to become dearer. High cost import goods then fuel inflation. Such a situation can be prevented by making the exchange rate fixed.

Disadvantages of fixed exchange rate system:

First, Speculation Encouraged:

In fact, uncertainty and, hence, speculative activities, tend to get a boost even under the fixed exchange rate system. Under a fixed rate system, if a country faces huge balance of payments deficit then the possibility of speculation gets brightened. If the speculators can guess that such balance of payments deficit will persist in the days ahead and the authority may go for a cut in foreign exchange rate, then these people will be more enthusiastic to sell domestic currencies in the foreign exchange market.

If such sale of home currencies continues for a longer period, the central bank will then be forced to reduce exchange rate, instead of keeping it at the old fixed rate. Under the circumstance, speculators go on buying home currencies where exchange rates have been reduced. This will make these people earn a profit.

Second, Adequacy of Foreign Exchange Reserves:

For the effectiveness of a stable exchange rate, the necessary condition is the adequacy of holding, foreign exchange reserves. Poor developing countries find it difficult to maintain an adequate volume of foreign exchange reserves. Speculators then anticipate currency devaluation in advances if balance of payments needs to be corrected. Before 1970, fixed exchange rate, in fact, prevailed because of low volume of global trade and, hence, low volume of foreign exchange reserves.

Third, Internal Objectives of Growth and Full Employment Sacrificed:

When countries experience large and persistent deficits or 'fundamental disequilibrium' in balance of payments, they are down with the foreign exchange reserves. Countries then opt for devaluation of their currencies and take some internal measures to reduce their deficits.

These harsh internal measures tend to contract economies. But the fallouts of these measures are rising prices and rising unemployment. These then reduce economic growth. Thus, fixed exchange rate, in the ultimate analysis, goes for currency depreciation that results in lower economic growth and higher unemployment coupled with high inflation, the two most undesirable and unpleasant macro- economic variables not liked by anyone.

Fourth, International Competitive Environment Bypassed:

The continuous changes in international competitive environment do not get reflected under the fixed exchange rate system. Thus, to make the home product more competitive in the foreign market, what is required is the change in domestic economic policies so that the country's export products get a larger foothold in the foreign market. In other words, the fixed exchange rate system fails to gloss over the international competitive environment.

This kind of exchange rate developed after World War II. The International Monetary Fund set up by the Bretton Woods Agreement of 1944 came into operation in March 1947. The period 1947-1971 came to be known as 'fixed but adjustable exchange rate system', 'par value system', the 'pegged exchange rate system' or the 'Bretton Woods System'.

INFLATION AND VARIABLE INTEREST 13

As the Bretton Woods System collapsed, several stop-gap measures were taken but uncertainty and confusion in the exchange rate systems continued. Ultimately, in 1973, the world's exchange rate system came to be known as the 'managed floating'—in the sense that currencies tend to float freely in the foreign exchange market.

Advantages of Floating Exchange Rates:

First, Automatic Stabilization:

Any disequilibrium in the balance of payments would be automatically corrected by a change in the exchange rate. For example, if a country suffers from a deficit in the balance of payments then, other things being equal, the country's currency should depreciate.

This would make the country's exports cheaper, thus increasing demand, while at the same time making imports expensive and decreasing demand. The balance of payments equilibrium would therefore be restored. On the contrary, a balance of payments surplus would be automatically eliminated through a change in the exchange rate.

Second, Freeing Internal Policy:

Under the floating exchange rate system, the balance of payments deficit of a country can be rectified by changing the external price of the currency. In the country if a fixed exchange rate policy is adopted, then reducing a deficit could involve a general deflationary policy for the whole economy, resulting in unpleasant consequences such as unemployment and idle capacity.

Thus, a floating exchange rate allows a government to pursue internal policy objectives such as full employment growth in the absence of demand-pull inflation without external constraints such as debt burden or shortage of foreign exchange.

Third, Absence of Crisis:

The periods of fixed exchange rates were frequently characterized by crisis as too much pressure was put on central bank to devalue or revalue the country's currency. However, the central bank that devalued a currency by giving out too much of it would soon either stop or run out of it.

INFLATION AND VARIABLE INTEREST 15

Similarly, the central banks that revalued a currency by giving out too little of it in exchange for other currencies would soon be flooded with that currency as it would get relatively large amounts of other currencies. Under floating exchange rate system such changes occur automatically. Thus, the possibility of international monetary crisis originating from exchange rate changes is automatically eliminated.

Fourth, Management:

J. E. Meade has pointed out that under the floating exchange rates system national governments enjoy considerable discretion. To be more specific, governments are free to manipulate the external value of their currency to their own advantage.

Fifth, Flexibility:

Changes in world trade since the first oil crisis of 1973 have caused great changes in the values of currencies. How these could have been dealt with under a system of fixed exchange rate is not yet clear.

Sixth, Avoiding Inflation:

John Beard Shaw has argued that, "A floating exchange rate helps to insulate a country from inflation elsewhere. In the first place, if a country were on a fixed exchange rate then it would 'import' inflation by way of higher import prices. Secondly, a country with a balance of payments surplus and a fixed exchange rate would tend to 'import' inflation from countries that have balance of payments deficit."

Seventh, Lower Reserves:

Finally, floating exchange rates should mean that there is hardly any need to maintain large reserves to develop the economy. These reserves can therefore be fruitfully used to import capital goods and other items in order to promote faster economic growth.

Disadvantages of Floating Exchange Rates:

First, Uncertainty:

The very fact that currencies change in value from day to day introduces a large element of uncertainty into trade. A seller may not be quite sure of how much money he will receive when he sells goods abroad. Some of this uncertainty may be reduced by companies buying currency ahead in forward exchange contracts.

Second, Lack of Investment:

The uncertainty introduced by floating exchange rates may discourage direct foreign investment, for example investment by multinational companies.

Third, Speculation:

The day-to-day fluctuations in exchange rates may encourage speculative movements of 'hot money' from country to country, thereby causing more and more exchange rate fluctuations.

Fourth, Lack of Discipline:

The need to maintain an exchange rate imposes a lack of discipline upon the national economy. It is quite possible that with a floating exchange rate such short-run problems as domestic inflation may be ignored until they have created crisis situations.

In July 1944, the Bretton Woods Agreement introduced the concept of pegged currencies against the US dollar that was tied to the price of gold. In 1973, the system collapsed following a sharp appreciation in the price of the US dollar that raised a red flag with respect to exchange rates and the ties of the US dollar to the price of gold. From 1973 until today, countries are free to choose their exchange agreement.

Nobody can judge which exchange rate monetary system is best, because both have advantages and disadvantages while the exchange rate monetary system for a country is chosen according to its traditions and culture.

Export or No Export?

Depreciation of currency is good news for an exporter because this means he is going to export his merchandise cheaper than before if he is looking forward to making profits in his local currency. For example, if before depreciation of currency one dollar is equal to two local currencies and an exporter sells something for four local currencies then that something is going to be exported for two dollars. If after depreciation of currency one dollar has become equal to four local currencies, then that something is going to be exported for one dollar. That's if that exporter is still selling it for four local currencies.

For United States, if before depreciation of currency one dollar is equal to two foreign currencies and an exporter sells something for two dollars then that something is going to be exported for four foreign currencies. If after depreciation of currency one dollar has become equal to one foreign currency, then that something is going to be exported for two foreign currencies.

This is cool for exporters, makes them export more merchandise theoretically but there is a tough competition out there for exporters, selling for less means you sell garbage for some consumers. Of course, competition gets even worse when currency appreciation takes place.

On the other hand, less imported goods lead to slow production as there's not always a fast way to get raw material from local companies. Because, in most cases a buyer must wait in line to get his raw material from a local company while an exporter has a warehouse full of that raw material already.

For example, there's an American city A that makes cigarettes and an American city B that farms tobacco and a Chinese city C that farms tobacco too, what makes city A buy tobacco from city C not city B: First, it's still too early to harvest tobacco right now! Second, there is no trade route between city A and city B because there's no passable routs between the two cities or because it's not profitable for the carrier to transport goods between the two cities.

INFLATION AND VARIABLE INTEREST 21

Here comes the need for some trade agreements like NAFTA or the new one USMCA that replaces NAFTA, one of the benefits of such agreements is to open a new trade route for a quicker production rate.

What's NAFTA? The North American Free Trade Agreement, which eliminated most tariffs on trade between Mexico, Canada and the United States, went into effect on Jan. 1, 1994. NAFTA's purpose is to encourage economic activity between North America's three major economic powers.

Keep in mind that the increase in imported goods amount weakens the economy, theoretically the amount of exported goods must exceed the amount of imported goods for strong economy. Also, trade agreements are not a complete solution for slow production rate as the lack of raw material has influence on production rate too, less imported goods mean most of the raw materials is consumed locally even before production.

As explained, going for more exported goods and less imported goods is not the magical economic remedy.

I have read about the new USMCA, but I did not find any paragraph about the wall or even the word "wall", this puts this one-million-dollar question: **But Where is the wall?** If you can find an answer, please contact me and you will be rewarded!

The Importance of Inflation Rate

Inflation occurs when there is a sustained increase in the general price level. Traditionally high inflation rates are damaging to an economy. High inflation creates uncertainty and can wipe away the value of savings. However, most Central Banks target an inflation rate of 2%, suggesting that low inflation can have various advantages to the economy. Some economists even argue we should target a higher inflation rate during periods of economic stagnation.

The Advantages of Inflation:

First, Deflation is very harmful:

During a prolonged period of deflation and very low inflation, the Japanese economy has suffered lower growth because of deflationary pressures. When prices are falling people are reluctant to spend money because they are concerned that prices will be cheaper in the future, therefore, they keep delaying purchases. Also, deflation increases the real value of debt and reduces the disposable income of individuals who are struggling to pay off their debt. When people take on a debt like a mortgage, they generally expect an inflation rate of 2% to help erode the value of debt over time. If this inflation rate of 2% fails to materialize, their debt burden will be greater than expected.

Second, Moderate inflation enables adjustment of wages:

It is argued a moderate rate of inflation makes it easier to adjust relative wages. For example, if average wages are rising due to moderate inflation, it is easier to increase the wages of productive workers wages, unproductive workers can have their wages frozen which is effectively a real wage cut. If we had zero inflation, we could end up with more real wage unemployment, with firms unable to cut wages to attract workers.

Third, Inflation enables adjustment of relative prices:

Like the last point, moderate inflation makes it easier to adjust relative prices. This is particularly important for a single currency like the Euro zone. Southern European countries like Italy, Spain and Greece became noncompetitive, leading to large current account deficit. Because Spain and Greece cannot devalue in the single currency, they are having to cut relative prices to regain competitiveness. With very low inflation in Europe, this means they must cut prices and cut wages, which causes lower growth due to effects of deflation. If the Euro zone had moderate inflation, it would be easier for southern Europe to adjust and resume being competitive without resorting to deflation.

Fourth, Inflation can boost growth:

At times of very low inflation the economy may be stuck in a recession. Arguably targeting a higher rate of inflation can enable a boost in economic growth. This view is controversial. Not all economists would support targeting a higher inflation rate. However, some would target higher inflation, if the economy was stuck in a prolonged recession.

For example, the Euro zone has had a very low inflation rate in 2013-14, and this has corresponded to very weak economic growth and very high unemployment.

Disadvantages of Inflation:

Inflation is usually considered to be a problem when the inflation rate rises above 2%. The higher the inflation, the more serious a problem it is. In extreme circumstances hyperinflation can wipe away people's savings and cause great instability, for example Germany 1920s, Hungary 1940s, Zimbabwe 200s. However, in a modern economy, this kind of hyperinflation is rare. Usually inflation is accompanied with higher interest rates, so savers do not see their savings wiped away.

Inflationary growth tends to be unsustainable leading to a damaging period of boom and bust economic cycles. For example, the UK saw high inflation in the late 1980s, but this economic boom was unsustainable and when the government tried to reduce inflation, it led to the recession of 1990-92.

Inflation tends to discourage investment and long-term economic growth. This is because of the uncertainty and confusion that is more likely to occur during periods of high inflation. Low inflation is said to encourage greater stability and encourage firms to take risks and invest.

Inflation can make an economy noncompetitive. For example, a relatively higher rate of inflation in Italy can make Italian exports noncompetitive, leading to lower aggregate demand and lower economic growth. This is particularly important for countries in the Euro-zone because they can't devalue to restore competitiveness.

Inflation leads to a fall in the value of money. This makes savers worse off if inflation is higher than interest rates. High inflation can lead to a redistribution of income in society. Often it is pensioners who lose out most from inflation. This is particularly a problem if inflation is high and interest rates are low.

How to Limit Inflation?

Now let's discuss how to limit inflation and avoid deflation at the same time? As explained before revaluation of currency is refused because it might lead to deflation. That's to say revaluation of currency leads prices to drop. This price drop might lead to deflation which should be avoided.

On the other side, devaluation of currency weakens economy, that's to say the more your currency is valuable the stronger economy you have. Besides economists can't keep devaluation of local currency until it reaches zero of course.

This concludes that both devaluation of currency and revaluation of currency is a refused strategy to limit inflation. So, what can limit inflation? Controlling the interest rate is a known strategy to limit inflation. How?

Let's first discuss the effect of interest rate on inflation rate, simply if a bank increases its interest rate, people will rush to make savings deposits at that bank for

INFLATION AND VARIABLE INTEREST   29

more profits. Then those people will not have much to spend, so they will not buy large quantities. This means less demand on goods, so prices will decrease and that means inflation rate goes low.

That's to say, interest rate increase leads to inflation rate decrease. On the other hand, if a bank decreases its interest rate, people will not be interested, they will withdraw their savings deposits looking for somewhere else for more profits. Then people will have much to spend, so they will buy large quantities. This means more demand on goods, so prices will increase and that means inflation rate goes high. That's to say, interest rate decrease leads to inflation rate increase.

This concludes that, there is an inverse relationship between inflation rate and interest rate. This inverse relationship can be explained simply: cash goes to the bank, so inflation rate decreases while cash goes out of the bank, so inflation rate increases. On the other hand, the relationship between interest rate and inflation is unknown since the effect of interest rate on prices happens over time.

The strategy usually used nowadays to limit inflation is to devalue local currency to increase inflation rate. On the opposite side, economists increase interest rate to decrease inflation rate. Economists should keep increase and decrease inflation rate as needed for the economy to run smoothly. Unfortunately, this strategy might lead to extremely depreciate local currency in a way that's unnecessary. That's to say they can achieve the same inflation rate level with a higher local currency value.

Inflation Rate Control Loop

In the simplest type of an automatic control loop, a controller compares a measured value of a process with a desired set value and processes the resulting error signal to change some input to the process, in such a way that the process stays at its set point despite disturbances. This set point is usually the desired set value.

How to apply this control loop to control inflation rate? The controller mentioned above should be the central bank. Now, "Inflation Rate Control Loop" theory is as follows:

The central bank should compare the current measured value of inflation rate with a desired set value and calculates the resulting interest rate to change the inflation rate in such a way that the inflation rate stays at its desired set value despite disturbances.

The above paragraph is an economic theory called "Inflation Rate Control Loop" theory. That's nice, now we will discuss the obstacles that make applying this theory difficult.

This theory implies raising and reducing interest rate according to the desired value of inflation rate, of course increasing interest rate will naturally decrease inflation rate, but there is a risk of bankruptcy as the calculated interest rate might cause a cash shortage for a bank.

This is the first obstacle, the second obstacle is decreasing interest rate doesn't insure increasing inflation rate, as some people will withdraw their savings deposits and others won't. What really does matter is that we need cash to walk out of the bank to increase inflation! Yes, that's what does really matter.

That's a problem in American economy, some economists think that lowering the interest rate is quite enough to increase inflation rate but that's wrong that's not enough as some savings deposits will be still in the bank, what really increases inflation rate is to make cash walk out of the bank.

The first part of this theory which is decreasing inflation rate is quite easy, but it has a risk of bankruptcy

INFLATION AND VARIABLE INTEREST   33

while the second part which is increasing the inflation rate by a calculated certain amount has an obstacle which is decreasing interest rate doesn't insure increasing inflation rate.

Of course, devaluation of currency is enough to increase inflation rate, but we want to avoid devaluation of currency as both devaluation of currency and revaluation of currency is a refused strategy to limit inflation, as explained before.

Really, we want this theory to compensate for devaluation of currency as a disturbance not as a method to increase inflation as it is the case nowadays, because devaluation of currency weakens economy as explained before. That's the new feature of this theory.

Let's start with how to avoid bankruptcy. For a bank to pile up cash to avoid bankruptcy, a bank should sell a variable interest rate savings deposits to his customers. But why? Because this theory depends on interest rate as a compensator for inflation rate's deviation of the set value, so the interest rate is always a variable that's calculated periodically according to the desired set value of inflation rate.

In this case, selling a variable interest rate savings deposits to customers, insures that a certain amount of cash is always in the bank whatever the calculated interest rate is. The more a bank sells those variable interest rate savings deposits the more it avoids bankruptcy.

A bank should sell those variable interest rate savings deposits to customers as needed, they should be sold in case that bank has a cash shortage, after all, we don't want all savings deposits to be a variable interest rate savings deposit!

But those variable interest rate savings deposits have no effect on inflation rate, they are just to avoid bankruptcy. Why? Because in this case of variable interest rate savings deposits neither cash walks out of the bank nor cash walks in the bank, they are just to pile up some cash to avoid bankruptcy.

Really, it's always the case that variable interest rate savings deposits have no effect on inflation rate, that's why you the reader might not have heard about it, be-

INFLATION AND VARIABLE INTEREST

cause it's the fixed interest rate savings deposits that affect inflation rate.

Those variable interest rate savings deposits can be for long term, no problem, as they don't affect inflation rate, but they can't be for short term as this would increase the risk of bankruptcy.

Now how to make decreasing interest rate effective to increase inflation rate? We want to push that cash out of the bank! a bank should sell a fixed interest rate short term savings deposits to its customers. But why? Because a fixed interest rate savings deposit affects inflation rate, but why short term? Because this theory depends on interest rate as a compensator for inflation rate's deviation of the desired set value, so the interest rate is always a variable that's calculated periodically according to the desired set value of inflation rate. So, interest rate can't be a fixed value for a long time really.

In this case, selling a fixed interest rate short term savings deposits to customers, insures that customers will spend their savings deposits when interest rate goes low as their high fixed interest rate savings deposits have expired. This low interest rate accompanied by customers' money, which they used to buy savings deposits, is back in their accounts and will encourage them to spend their savings. This lets cash walk out of the bank.

On the other hand, a high interest rate accompanied by customers' money, which they used to buy savings deposits, is back in their accounts and will encourage them to buy those high fixed interest rate savings deposits. This lets cash walk in the bank. This high interest rate should be greater than the interest rate of variable interest rate savings deposits.

How long is this short term? This short term should be synchronized with the period of changing the interest rate, for example, if interest rate changes monthly then this short term cannot exceed one month. Because, the theory needs at least most of fixed interest rate savings deposits to be expired at the time which interest rate changes. That money, which was used to buy savings deposits, goes back in costumers' accounts when it's time to set a new value for interest rate, that's to compensate

INFLATION AND VARIABLE INTEREST 37

for the current inflation rate's deviation of the desired set value.

This theory introduces an alternative way for devaluation of currency to increase inflation rate, which is important for Euro zone. So, in this theory a bank should have the majority of its savings deposits as a long-term variable interest deposit to provide cash, so it will not have cash shortage, and in the same time it should have some of its savings deposits as a short-term fixed interest deposit to control inflation rate.

Benefits of "Inflation Rate Closed Loop" Theory: This closed loop should be immune to currency fluctuations as it does compensate for both slight currency depreciation and appreciation automatically. It's also immune to bankruptcy as a bank should have most of its savings deposits as a long-term variable interest savings deposit to provide cash. There's no need to extremely devalue local currency in a way that's unnecessary. That's to say the desired inflation rate level can be achieved by a higher local currency value than if this theory is not used. This theory makes a stronger economy by maintaining the real value of the local currency. There is no need usually for local currency devaluation.

Finally, I wish for someone to find this theory useful!

Don't miss out!

Visit the website below and you can sign up to receive emails whenever Mohammed Azzam publishes a new book. There's no charge and no obligation.

https://books2read.com/r/B-A-QOZG-LHKV

BOOKS 2 READ

Connecting independent readers to independent writers.

Also by Mohammed Azzam

Inflation and Variable Interest
Virtual Reality and Augmented Reality Safety Rules
Known Facts of Time Travel

Watch for more at https://books2read.com/ap/R3Lm35/Mohammed-Azzam.

About the Author

Hello, my name is Mohammed Azzam :
E-Mail : smartspecies@hotmail.com
Occupation : software-engineer.
Education : Faculty of Engineering - I have a B.A. in Automatic Control Engineering.
Certification :
Oracle PL/SQL Developer Certified Associate (OCA)
Oracle Forms Developer Certified Professional (OCP)
Oracle Database: SQL Certified Expert (OCE) Oracle Certified Professional, Java SE 6 Programmer (SCJP)
Oracle Certified Expert, Java EE 6 Web Component

Developer (SCWCD)
Read more at https://books2read.com/ap/R3Lm35/Mohammed-Azzam.

www.ingramcontent.com/pod-product-compliance
Lightning Source LLC
Chambersburg PA
CBHW030515220526
45464CB00006B/2806